How you can help

First steps with ladybird *abc* helps children to recognise the letters of the alphabet and the sounds they make by linking them with colourful photographs of familiar and interesting objects.

- As you look at the book together, encourage your child to say the name of each letter and then practise saying the sound that the letter makes (**a** as in **a**pple, **b** as in **b**us)

- Encourage him* to trace over the letter shapes with each finger

There are lots of other ways you can help your child learn about the alphabet. He could form letter shapes out of play dough, or write them with finger paints or sand. Try spotting different letters at home and on trips out, or play I-spy using the letter sound.

*To avoid the clumsy 'he/she',
the child is referred to throughout as 'he'.*

Ladybird would like to thank Priscilla Hannaford, freelance editor on this series.

Published by Ladybird Books Ltd
A Penguin Company
Penguin Books Ltd, 80 Strand London WC2R 0RL, UK
Penguin Books Australia Ltd, Camberwell, Victoria, Australia
Penguin Books (NZ) Ltd, Private Bag 102902, NSMC, Auckland, New Zealand

7 9 10 8 6

first steps with ladybird

abc

by Lesley Clark
photography by Garie Hind
illustrations by Terry Burton

alligator

ambulance

astronaut

apple

b

bus

banana

ball

baby

comb

cat

car

carrot

d

duck

dog

dinosaur

doll

exit

exit

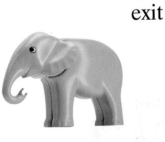

elephant   envelope

egg

fork

fan

feather

fish

goat

guitar

gate

girl

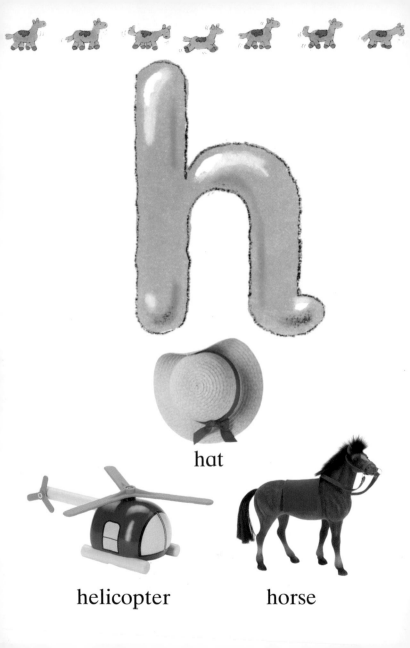

h

hat

helicopter   horse

house

invitation

jigsaw

k

kite

kangaroo

keys

king

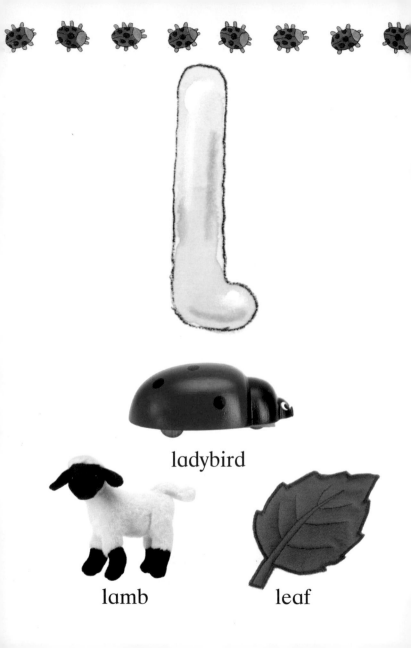

ladybird

lamb

leaf

lion

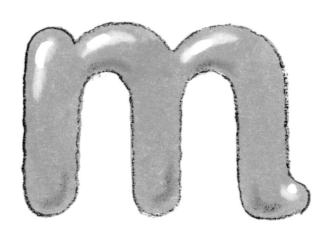

mouse

motorbike

monkey

mug

n

nurse

orange

pencil

penguin

pineapple

painting

quack! quack!

queen

rocket

seal

soap

sandwich

socks

toothbrush

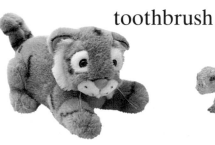

tiger

tortoise

telephone

underwear

upside down

up

umbrella

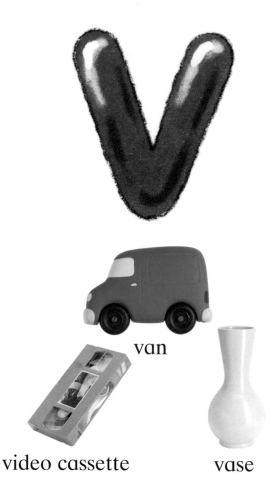

van

video cassette

vase

vet

watch

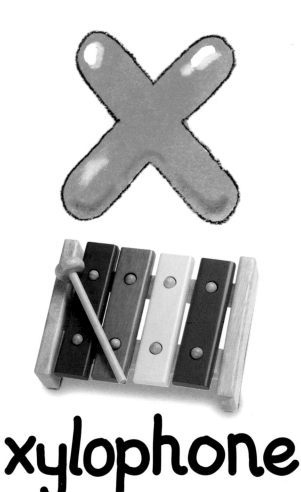

xylophone

y

yo-yo